American Sweethearts:

~~Thoughts of~~

~~the~~

~~Lost & Found~~

A Poetry Book
By: Mario Guzman Jr.

"Telling on yourself

is the only you wanna escape"

-     Future (I'm on one)

Copyright

Dedication

This one is dedicated to me.
I need to fuel my ambition as a writer.
I'm kidding.
This is for my Beezley Hills family.
Tiger town.
Always.
Thank you for reading this, (I can really use the money).

Also, a special thank you to the kindest person I know, Nway.
I have the privilege of calling you, my friend. You made it
possible for me to start, and continue this writing endeavor,
while my time in Los Angeles.
I will always be grateful.

Table of Contents

Poetry
Written by me

Translated by you

☐

Why?

Because of love

Because I fell for it

Because of hate

Because I fall for it

Because I want it

Because I need it

Because despite it all

Became my everything

Because in the end

Becomes my *why*

☐

Light

Candles in torches

Torches in cigarettes

Matches in pockets

Chivalry still exists

A man with his love, he's born with

A woman with hate, she's learned it

Once upon a time, like tomorrow

Cupid, and Robin hood got together

Hourglasses, Apple watches

Pebble steps, number highlights

Does this sound familiar....

Pool gambles, coin chances, and life poker

Says it doesn't

☐

American apples

Down the grass isle

Lay thousands of seeds

Spring has sprung forward

Clocking the needle hours earlier

Dawn spreads over hundreds of trees

Exposing the minutes

Agriculture workers

Scurrying, to help the apple orchard

A few months ago, during winter

Her branches were trimmed off naked

Needed to be bare

Harvest must be delivered on every home table

I thinned apple trees as a kid

Then as a teen

Growing to adolescent

Every time, for the hope of American breakfast

Working, maintaining the buds

Five or six in a bunch

I would cut off at least three

Dropping aborted seed bunches, on the grass isles

Ladder steps at elevator speed checks

Rooting for life in between the leaves

Seeds of many 'dreamers', dreams

Dried on those isles

On those isles made of straight vessels

Those isles reminding us not all dreams become *purpose*

Those isles shivering innocent conscience

Those isles forming straight perfect apples

☐

Ray-Ban

I look shady cool

I look smart unlike you fools

I should have been named Steve Erkel

I look cocky like crows

I mock life like bills

I fit spot on against heat waves

In front of these lenses

Like I was banned against sunrays

So, yea…

Ray-Ban's was a good investment

Baby member

Running around the playground

Tagging soft touches

Like innocent consent

Choosing each other to trust

Us, our family

We once were surprised to wake up in this world

Mom, dad, are busy

Us kids didn't mind, we could hold each other's hand

When one of us left

The other was tough, and the other had a bandage

Another may have been confused

Another sad

Another so happy

Regardless *we* babies evolved as us today

Us, our family

☐

☐

Jasmine flowers

I wanted caffeine

Instead, I found she

Sweet like powder white, pink, yellow packets

Her lips couldn't give me diabetes

My drowsiness needs her coffee taste every morning

Whipped cream of her lipstick

Wakes me, as soon as I sip

Holding her cup molding palms and fingers

Hot, then cooling into heartwarming sign language

Sexy is she

I wish I was valiant

The least I can do

Is buy these bouquet bundle thoughts of you

With a letter note from me

Attach with a p.s. 'wink'

☐

Story

Remember that time I sat you down to listen to me

It was ten years ago

Just like right now

It was us

Like family

Holidays

Like unborn

It was like fairy pillows

Loose tooth's

It was a screen of beautiful emotions

It was exotic

But let's keep this pg-13

Remember yesterday

When I kissed you until tomorrow

It was us teenagers

Driving without a license

It was back allies

Foggy windows

It is…

Like closed eyes

Never forgetting your picture

☐

Humor

Did you know…

That a monkey that wins a game

Is, called a "Chimp-pion"

Did you know…

That the straw broke the camel's back

Because it was a jackass

Did you know…

2 plus 2 equals 42

Because I lost my checkbook

Did you know…

That we keep breaking each other's heart

Because neither of us are doctors

Did you know…

That I write this

Because I can't have a sense of humor

Acura TL

I bought her when my Cherry Chevy broke down

A stupid boulder broke my 03' Cavaliers under oil pan

The loud thump had me running outside to find tracks make
of ink

The next day I woke up and went to Wenatchee

Stupid salesman, seduced and sold her to me

Signing me to a 12 old white sedan

With a contract agreeing to absurd numbers

It hurt to sign my autograph to this fancy salesman

Today he must know

I crushed his Acura TL deal

Crashing the shit out the front bumper

Drunk, as fuck, I went out

Only to suddenly hit to a halt

Behind some California driver

☐

Babysitting

I wanted to be a parent

So, I applied at a nursing home

My cousin said

'They'll give you a job

Once you learn to change diapers'

I laughed the inside joke

My girl and I were still virgin

We weren't even at 'baseball plate', conversations

But lately I felt the heat of our hormones home running

All backed up in my feelings

At night, I imagined us coming all over the back seat

I had to step up and be ready

In case we had bastard children

Because I was too young to get married

Shit, I wasn't even in love

So, I told myself...

Now, doing nursing assistant jobs

For over ten years

I think about how I thought a handicapped person looked blue

Boy I was wrong

For the first time

I see the *gravity* of my situation

Healthcare jobs

This job has me saying weird things like,

"In the mist of this flatulence aroma, I couldn't help but to notice you're too pretty to be here."

Street foods

Have you ever eaten roadkill?

I have

That chicken shouldn't have been in the driveway

Dear Cousin

Mountain View school in Quincy

Will always be a special memory

That first grade experience against a bully

You were there for me

I remember sounding weak against this ugly kid

I told him if he didn't back up, I would tell my cousin

He didn't

So, I did what was best

And told you

I cannot remember your exact words to him

Standing up against that shithead

But I felt safe when you were there for me

I will never forget you staring down at him

On top of the wooden playset

Threatening consequences if he talked to me without manners again

Years later I found a new bully

This time disguised as a beautiful woman

How those feelings confused ugly situations

Revolving around blank love bullets

Which I had to take

It hurt more than you will ever know

But seeing you cry that morning

In Big Bend

Broke me

I never meant to take her side, over you cousin

I'm sorry

Please know I was never an angry kid

Never a curious teen

But now as adolescent, I get mad for being too free

My regrets, my betrayal in college

Leads me to haunted houses in Los Angeles...

That small town in the Apple State

Grew a pair on me

Now sharing your spirit through me

In The Golden State

I take that anger you have now resided

Family comes first on this world's playset

Fondest memory of family though,

I have for sure

Soft blood

Know that I can never forget what I saw in you

Being angry because bitches around you wouldn't comply

We were small weren't we

But me being a boxer

You, being a crash survivor

Fighting for our lungs

All these years later...

All these years later we calmed down

Like palm trees shadowing our brows

We continue to see more wrinkles, white hair, white lies

Our kids continue growing up, unlike us

And that's for the best

Before back then, on the playground

Just know Cuz, that I know

It wasn't safe without you

My favorite person

Hey Shelby

How are you?

How's your husband?

How are your two sons and daughter?

Are you a nurse yet?

Do you still get offended when people say,

"Tough titty said the kitty when the milk went dry"

Do you still say "Whoo-ell", with smirking eyes?

Do you still have those scrubs I bought you?

Do you still think of me?

I do

Anyways, 30 was around the corner

Remembering you had promised to split a 6 of Corona

With me

That weird person that was a nuisance in your life

I am sorry by the way

And in case you have decided to take a raincheck

It's okay

Now I'm too far away

☐

EBT

The gasoline clerk looked annoyed

The man couldn't find his government card

He searched around his pockets

Stalling with excuses

Of hiding his card from the homeless

Finally, in his back pocket he finds it

"Here it is!" he yells the teller

When it's my turn to pay

He rings the beer

Without even looking at my shaved face

Still annoyed

Murmuring something about EBT

I tell this foreigner a foreign truth

"Here in this nation, we are all children of the government"

☐

Charles Bukowski

My hero

I wish I had known his name

Back in grade years

When asked by the school teacher

It's okay

I'm glad I found him at this age

Because back then

He just wouldn't make sense

☐

Play me some blues

Lavender wounds at 3a.m. start bleeding

Clogging into morning blues

Violets mixed with midnight colors

Paint a pondering picture of you

Somewhere out there I know you're lost

Knowing broken hearts bring out

Some gem stolen moments

Giving reason to my veins and arteries

To keep digging reasons to find you

My wrists are tired

My hope burns in fire

My voice sounds no more desire

My muscles ground to the pebbles

My head can only dream

My thoughts I saw during strength

My breathing from death to *fantasy*

Your lipstick kissing imprints, *I Love You*

Accelerating riding dreams about you

Garnet seductive dress wrapped around you

Floors my steps, slippery to you

Clumsy, wobbly, like maybe I should slow down

Calm down

Before my chest speeds past

Your palms up, stop sign

Derision

I have to try

I just have to

I didn't know

Long ago

I made a decision to fail

I was best at that

I was…

I was…

Today, I am

☐

Tired

Sleepy mixed with drinking

Is dangerous for the roads

Exhausted mixed with liquor

Is damning to the soul

Frustrations mixed with prescriptions

Is deafening to the voice

Necessity mixed with materials

Is the definition of my times

Traffic

L. A. drivers remind me of home

Washington State

Cruising teen slow

I-90 to Seattle

Then back to Moses Lake

70 speeds on the freeway

Reminded me, of me

Carefully respecting animal, pedestrians

But this time I play Kurt Cobain music

Speeding punk-rock miles with my foot

Passing yellow bricks and dead squirrels

Vehicles begin looking like turtles

"Just crank up to 'rabbit, like lawnmowers" I scream

"Or just get the fuck off the road!"

Propaganda

When all the movies, I love

When all the people, I love

When all the music, I love

When all feelings, I love

When it all starts to make sense

Is when all

Starts falling apart

Posters

Driving down Sunset Boulevard

I see movies, people, music on the buildings

Vacation is now somewhat my nightmare

As Hollywood at night visits my dreams

With extra strangers seducing me

Rehearsing written role-playing sheets

Voicing inspiration quotes for the year

Accepting streaming like family

The lights in front of screens are beauty

I can't complain about those companies

Warner Bros, Universal studios, Disney

And all the below

This movie I saw

Made me hate to be part of love

Huddling teams of special needs

Speaking different languages

Like the Holy Ghost talking

Nothing around is incompetent

But the mistakes of, camera-action

The download is successful

When the enemy visual continues coming

Propaganda respects a halt

Nothing, and I mean nothing

Is greater than the God of my plans

But isn't that what Hitler said,

Country, after country

Running them down, like world tours

Stepping, stomping, strapped

Marching forward like Spring comes in March

Nothing is about to stop a flag made of mutation

Evolving bulldozer men into Pitbull mean

Killing the screams made of birds, with broken wings

Crashing the fumes into hills made of dreams

Fire lights up like fireworks

An independence man better write up

Bullets over me, near, and through

They poke a hole, opening new wounds

Parking my thumb on the trigger

Squeezing the pedal

If the race starts at the finish…

But I can't finish until all the dishes are clean

Momma doesn't allow friends after dusk

Chores, homework, must be done

Once poppa gets home

Once poppa takes off his shoes

Once poppa is sound asleep

Now grounded kids like me can wake up

Like wet worms underground

Like excuses full of cement soil

Printing the concrete, fingerprints of the wanted

Fresh only once like before being stoned

Rocking now like fossils

Better use this for fuel

After a chorus of delusion

An expulsion of prompt newsfeed

Doesn't go past this finger, no way

The index thumbtacked down like Jesus in the Bible

A line can't be crossed

But via envious middle whispers

A 'fuck' comes across

This world is too easy to come in

Ears made of virgins

Make this whole new cycle spin into a new sphere

We can like it, or not

It won't matter, the influence deep in the core is a spiral

Twisting our souls around rollercoasters

Up and down, I swear

Is propaganda at its finest

Asking without wanting

Our deepest questions

Made of confusing answers

Just to sow your mouth into a puppet showbiz mantle

    ☐

Notebook

Scribble some mental notes

In case you forget

Who knows

Maybe tomorrow you can cash them

⊔

Girlfriends

Not too long ago

Like forever ago

I had a girlfriend

After fucking

She loved me

Taking me serious

After coming

She wanted me

Like no rubber for protection

Like no periods

Rather exclamations

For her

I'm deaf in my feelings

Talking excuses with nonsense

So instead, I let her go

Before boxed-in emotions label, "Fragile"

☐

Pain of loneliness

Overthinking and under thinking

Are our inner nemesis

A constant battle of healthy

Versus selfish arguments

Loud thoughts of *what if*

Whispers of *should I*

One day, I'll finish this…

☐

Walkie-talking

I'm going to show you a world that you don't belong in

One that will scare you

Frighten you

Eventually hate you

Listen to me carefully

Down these steps

You'll be put into a 'mind'

However, remember of why you're walking into this place

Remind yourself that being chosen comes with a pain

Keep your soul no matter if it comes with a burden

Yesterday your heart was kept

Tomorrow is paradise

Just keep getting through these minutes of lies

Today can be an end

Promise me to finish across your heartbeat line

With at least one grain of faith

Climax

Infinity reasons why tonight I need you

Why tonight of all nights

A full moon might have its eye wide open

Exposing sky light onto our closed eyes

As our lips intertwine

We find shuttles to our minds

Heavenly clouds

Passing beyond drug galaxies

Cruising past other world problems

Exotic feelings flying us towards the moon

Where I know I love you

Losing myself with you

Breathing exiting panic

Then trusting your, *shush...*

As our desired quest

Comes to an end

Your chest becomes my outer space helmet

Falling and falling, *landing somewhere*

It was so worth it...

Don't forget the feeling

As we descend down to earth

Self-reflection

I can never know this man

He looks like he had a stroke

Puffing smoke of the city

out his nose

Solid like statue

Pigeons mix with ravens

No one is throwing out bits of bread

No one dares to take a picture beside him

No one scares the flies around him

Yet everyone

Every person

Admires *his* shoulders

Of 'The Thinking Man' in Paris

X-mas

Poetry is for people with feelings unlike me

I'm like Rudolph's evil twin saying

"Fuck you Santa, give me coke to keep my nose red

Maybe a molly to keep jolly around these stupid kids"

For sure I continue putting liquor in my coffee everyday

To barely stay awake

Settle again for another year

At least my least favorite holiday pays

Even if I show up late

Attitude of a Grinch

Taking one last sip of coffee

Before clocking in

Going to work, and steal lonely memories

All day

☐

Paper hearts

Forever ago

Like not long ago

I was in love

Yes, you read right

This tiny person with a 7-foot ego

Had a girlfriend

That was close to a wife

Such is life…

We learn to take what we can get

But that's what I regret

Like come on

Who the fuck keeps a picture of their ex from 2009

Such is death…

Until the end came too soon

Like alpha's bitch

You don't know me

But get in line to cash paper paystubs

White lies don't make sense to me because

My voice has no color

What I see every day is ink on contracts

Before they're even read

So how about you sign your soul to me

Like an autograph

Let's just call this

A mutual contract x_____

☐

give up

T. R. Y.

Is my three-letter acronym of, try

It stands to mean

'Tomorrow Remembers Yesterday'

Today however I must try

Try and try

To take what's mine

Try and try

To figure out

T. R. Y.

Wrath

Now you're going to feel what you should have known

When you weren't here

I hate you

I died when you left me on 'Dead End' roads

Like really?

I was your son; you son of a bitch!

Look now, where the fuck I've ended

Of course, like always

You don't care

It's not like your father did either

You should have just accepted his death

No

Instead, you let me feel it

☐

Thief

Heists in movies look awesome

Poor people taking things that don't belong to them

That's badass

Then I meet real thieves

Their names are,

Alzheimer's and Dementia

☐

Ivan

My best friend, until he dropped out of middle school

Actually, just a friend after Michael

We were teenagers, when his older brother got shot

Shot, straight in the head, like an 'accident'

I was sorry...

After that, he just became mean

Becoming something, he chose not to see

Becoming a scientist, without a degree

"You do what you have to," was his motto,

'You don't know how this feels,' was his sorrow,

He was a thug that got robbed from friends and romance

Years later, when his younger brother died

I think he changed

His younger brother was a happy, goofy child

The heart of the family

And again, I was sorry

"The innocent die, by damned destiny lies"

I wish I could tell him

Thank God, he changed his name back to Peter

The elderly

Don't call them old hags

I warn you

Shit if you do, I'll punch you

I don't have children

But their eyes remind me of them

So don't mess with them

Because I'm their legal guardian

Just because I wasn't close to my grandparents

Doesn't mean I can't have them

7 to 11, or, 3 to 7, introduced me to many of them

I was 19, when it hurt to see an old friend

I called family die

Lifeless and purple

With eyes wide open

I shook them to wake up

But they didn't

Their eyes…

Whatever they saw in me

I'll never forget

p.s. a letter to heaven

"I got more things to tell you my friends"

☐

Angry

I forgot how to cry

Is my frown upside, or down?

I hope its sideways, curved in a smile

No need to be angry

Just enjoy your life

As if it's a stand-up comedy

☐

Dehydrated

Yellow eyes have my body missing my liver

An organ so important needed to dissect the pills

Red eyes have my body missing myself

I don't know if I was any good

Shadow alleys have me looking for my heart

I hope I was vital

Blue oceans have me missing my beer

That, I'm sure to be true

☐

Motivation

Look up, and memorize yourself through the mirror

Listen to your fingers as they taste your skin

Now point down holding your heart palpitations

The display in front of you

Is reflection of truth

You, and only you

About you, and only you

A life portrait

Painted as present, for you

Take time to sit down

Even if walking

Converse on lonely benches by yourself

Even if talking to family or strangers

To wonder of you

About you, then why you

You, and only you

Know that you, and only you

Defines life

Shooting stars

If the promise didn't fulfill

Get in a fight with the genie

His moon shaped lamp poured down the stars too rapid

Too fast

The galaxies fireflies dropped over the hill

Too fast...

Too fast...

I forgot my wish now

☐

Education

High school was a memory

In my mind of portraits

Mathematics, English, and Science

Should have been my favorite subjects

Rather instead

I took a course to learn about you

Your class of style was more intriguing and interesting

I did my best to study you

But still I got an 'F'

Forgive me

☐

Foreign

This country of immigrants

Was founded by Europeans

The Mayflower boat brought

Many children and adult drunkards

When they arrived in America

They found aliens called 'Native Americans'

On that first day

They shared a wild turkey

The next day they stole a tamed land

Ever since then

People like me

Keep trying to do the same

☐

Bermuda triangle

According to the air geologists

There is a triangle in the sky that sucks in planes

Drawing the atlas spooky

Chem-trailing a mist of mysteries

Leaving no debris in the ocean

Fuck, not ever their souls drowning

Forget the sharks even eating their bodies

Bermuda triangle must be a stationary UFO

Or…

Maybe the air triangle is a conspiracy

Like the dollar note

Maybe UFO stands for

"Universes Forgets Outliers"

Kind of like me

Kind of like, we

Kind of like

If you're reading this

Then you're weird too

Just don't get sucked up like a cow

By a triangle cloud

To then wake up

By an alien Shrek

Dissecting your polluted mind

Jon Jones

This man 'Bones' is a tough motherfucker

Getting inside a locked 8-sided fenced cage

Fighting a human cock fight

Ego like his sharp lethal frame

Too cocky, giving the word 'confidence'

A run for its definition

Wild fists and kicks

Skinny limbs, backspin elbows, and flying knees

With barbaric emotions

Style of a starving, spoiled superstar…

The baddest man on the planet was crowned at 23

Reigned and reigned, against the enemies

In front of his division

The world at his feet called him the 'kingpin' of the sport

Win after win was achieved

Pound for pound status amongst the 'greatest' was complete

A slot for the 'best' of all time was no longer in question
He had all that he needed, plus more
More than he wanted, plus more

Plus, the lust and demons
That come with being a
Pound for pound 'king'

Pain

That evening

The ride in town was a cold one

My body knew it

My mind sensed it

My heart felt it

That lonely drive with my ex

I was in so much pain

Because she was about to move on to the next

And *he* seemed great

Younger, taller, more mature than me

Questioning the deep abyss inside me

I think I will never climb up to love again...

Zombies

Running, running, running

Mouth waters counting dry seconds

Chasing life vessels fulfilling angry appetites

Scattered scary soulless survivors

Searching for the systems

Supposing serenity is meant to be an answer

But all that ceases as frightening steps

Become closer and closer

Brains of zombies

Hungry to eat flesh ideas

Crazy ready to rip meat off the bones

Thirsty to drink blood

Of the lost and confused

☐

Things you should never do

Break into somebody's car

Break into somebody's heart

Steal somebody's watch

Steal somebody's love

Take somebody's keys

Take somebody's dream

Stop somebody's rhythm

Stop somebody's breathing

Check somebody's mail

Check somebody's feelings

Kill somebody's story

Kill somebody's, *finale*

☐

2023

If you add up the digits

It equals lucky #7

This should be the year then

Dedicated to risk taking

These should be the times

Devoted to roll playing

Like Russian-roulette

Like truth or dare

Like let's find out if you love me or don't

Anyways

Last year for my birthday

I wished to be a gift

Tell me if my imagination

Has lived up to it

A fight for the age of love

Those two seconds

Behind the high school restrooms

Was all it took

My knees shook

And I fell in love

Those lips pasted on mine

Surprise kiss!

She planted on me

The woman of my nightmares

Was becoming my novel dream

What a moment

She stole the glory

Of love chasing

She wanted me

And I did her

However, her life revolved around a boyfriend

Proud families

People of dynasty

Too pretty

Her features, just couldn't feature me

I understood

Even being teenage young

Love is a marriage arrangement

Something parents had to be involved with

In my case, a case of lust

"You'll move on"

"And so will she"

Boy did she

Who was I kidding

Because now, I hate that kid in me

Decades later

I find my letters inside her palms

Raspy voice, I fight to say

"I'm kidding baby"

"I'll never forget that kiss, two seconds ago"

Politics

Power over man and woman

Comes nowadays from Wi-Fi

Through flat screens, tablets, phones

Most of you are medium studs

Nothing wrong

Matter of fact

The best of us all

The war is between

The poor and the rich

Greed against the needy

Battles of rattle snakes

Hissing the same language

We all wish we were in the middle

The American Dream

Just don't forget

Who's tugging the ropes to our death

Them or *we*

Cups of letting go

Petri dish feelings as an adult

Surrounds me with plates of leftover food

Midnight-walk nutrition

Thoughts by binge reasons

Regarding an inside clock

Left by previous lifecycles

When, letting go, became the price

Cheap, expensive, isn't for me to judge

But what I can quote, is a tea party scenario

Sit next to me

Have yourself tea leaves, or coffee, even weed

Let's have a comfortable, profound conversation

About you...

"Karma is a bitch, ain't it.", I believe

Believe that

Even though we're Christians

☐

French dinner in Laguna

Never was I ever expensive taste until…

One evening, the waiter brought the check

Imagine my shocking eyeballs

When dinner was worth a double shift workday

Regardless, she was worth it

So, I paid smoothly

Easy, like my wallet was growing money seeds

Indeed, my date that evening by the beach

Was gorgeous tall sexy

About five inches taller than me

I faced her breasts perfectly

I had met her at work

Hung out a few times

But fucked many

Let's just say maybe I wasn't tall enough

For a relationship

But she still gave me the ride of my life

Always giving me soon desserts

Waiting behind motel doors, and off phones

Where she has gone

After them many rendezvous

I don't know

Having cost me my time, plus overtime

I couldn't care to know bank statements

Anyways, she made my lips expensive for tasting

Far from myself

That Victoria secret ingredient of

American French kissing

When I fail

When I fail

I'm going to fail with pride

Too many times...

I can't see eye to eye

Can't see mind to mind

But could see heart to hate

Lust sleeping with lies

I need time

To rethink who killed me

One thought second ago

I was young

Growing minute old

Arthritis has me scribbling some poem

My fingers aren't as meaningful as before

When pinky swears weren't meant anymore

Dear to you...

Greatest hits

From Elvis Presley to Tupac

Oldies to rap

Between jazz, blues, rock

Hip-hop, R&B, reggae

50s music to the present

Every genre of the pop charts

Playing over again in my cassette player

Radio stations

Even boom-box

Growing up younger with cd players, mp3, and iPod

Then, revolutionizing music to my life adult

Years through phones and concerts

All those great awesome artists and songs

Don't compare to the one & only

My personal favorite

The Greatest Hits of

My perfect pictures

Locked inside a photo album

Virginity

My youth didn't agree with puberty

Pimple fumbles kept my focus pointing down at the notebook

Writing down the laws of my universe

Making up my world full of myself

Then when her name came along my sentences

I couldn't help but put her before commas

Never in the end periods

Her life and I became combined

Like love letters in a page

Like smooches stamped on my face

Like paraphrasing the latter to:

I lost my virginity to lust, but I kept my innocent love and heart to the one who matters now

☐

Zero-thousand zero-hundred and zero

If you're interested in my debit card pin code

You can have it

Its four lonely digits, all hugging each other

I tried making the numbers special

Like the year I was born in

Or the day I found out my reason

But it all backfired when my birth year

Felt me too old

Especially when I couldn't flashback any reasons

I also don't want the thousand pin number obvious

Like the hundreds of personal identification attachments

Like who's counting on me

Or keeping prayers tracking

Or promised outdated goals

Or yearly notebooks

Or agenda dates of winning and losing

Or engagement celebrations

Or specific days of offspring

Or, God forbid, a death date

Who's

to say

Four random digits

Amounting to my savings

Or maybe four special hugs

Times multiplication

Reasons my hourglass's quicksand

Made of rock-bottom love

Amount a way out of these bank statements

I wouldn't know

I just know I keep forgetting the pin code

☐

Championship belts

Just to be clear, I'm not envious

Of them machine looking human beings

Athletic freaks specifically, the pugilists

Those kids, teens, men and woman

Practicing perfecting the sweet science

Fist trading for fun

Or for a payday

Or for the love of pain

Trailing the sport, myself

Proving gusto and valiance

Violence inside the squared circle never made any sense

But I kept fighting ghosts inside friends, and foes

For controlled temperament excuses

Maybe I hung up the gloves too soon

Or waited too long

My face, fingers, back, legs, bones, suggest

A story of their own

Composed of sacred stars, scarring a monster

Night ceiling canvas during combat

I see myself far across the ring

Buried deep dead, inside somebody's mind

I dig rock-bottom deep, pulling hate out myself

Hitting back with fossil grit

Tired between the balance of a perfect squared circle

Hopping inside the ropes, I find a warrior true friend

By the end of the night

I couldn't commit to ring engagements

Because championship belts

Won't fit around my jeans

My waist is too sexy

And my face now, not too pretty

I'll keep this pride for now

Because I'm humorously jealous

Dangerous friends

Talk to me…

Express that mess, obsess-web tangles, around your thoughts

Take me deep, to the unseen memory windows

A sleepy mental view

Breakfast, perfect dining table, inside mom's kitchen's

How come fog, then begins to blanket you

With chills crawling along your arms hallways

With unseen doors opening elegant like four seasons

Foggy inside your mansions mind, but not clear outside your passions address's

This puzzle of life has riddles, not easy to evolve around them

I'm no counselor, but maybe I talk answers

Let me guess scenarios, to understand some issues

The devil tripped you

You fell for an angelic face

Feeling the need to pray for attention

"I need them for self-change, God, let me have it"

"Why doesn't life make any sense?"

"How come I'm happy when I'm away"

"Who can understand me, so I won't be alone"

Along those praying cries comes a most twisted, but charming soul near you

You listen, but still can't take me serious

Confused again, about being confused

Yet you hold on to humanity

Material expectations, expecting honorable status

Love, for the naïve

'I', keeps 'me', talking to 'myself'

One last ride

Into the jungle

Into the wilderness

Into the woods

Into the den

There, glowing eyes pitch black

Stare back

Claws, foggy teeth

Snarls of hearts screeching

Its tongue meant to savor mistakes

My wrongs became appetite

I want to fight back

But in killing the beast

I need to kill myself too

The wolf lunges

I sprawl beneath it

Stabbing my jab, into its heart

Squeezing tight

Bleeding from holding, with might

My right choice hand swings back

Clamping its tongue

OBEY MY ORDERS, you beast!!!

I must tame the *monster*, taking over my mind

☐

Legal vs Illegal

A doctor checkup these days is too expensive

At least my pay stubs claim

I consume legal bottles prescribed by illegal emotions

The difference is my sheep life is fed by gambling shepherds

Hoax landlords

Like politics, and lottery afflictions

Having nothing to do with me, but deciding my fate

Taking pleasure in my misunderstanding

Accepting box choices

Saluting the flag, even when the forefathers print dirty money

I can cry, laugh, hate, and live death in between

Those awkward sentimental photos of myself

Re-living parties within annoying neighbors

Not so natural to the calm

Before the storm begins brewing

That storm…

I wish it was forbidden

I pray to life, like last seconds

Hearing the Lord upset

Is like me being pissed

About nonsense, bullshit

Consequences, choosing mischievous

Sins vs, that moment

Making Heaven hate me

Unleashing Saints into my world

Tagging with, or against them

Taking chances vs, me, or against, I

By the way…

As your legal mind-voice lawyer

I must charge you

For reading this

☐

Motel thoughts

When addresses were hard to come by

I had made home, too many motel nights

Roaches, stains, cigarette smells, sex scratches

All became too transparent

Apparent to my invisible imagination

Deliberately attacking my soft spots

Along with booze and drugs

Committing to hate and love

Often enough to write about, ghosts on the wall

Broken puzzle letters in clues expressed by graffiti

I can't sleep because I'm not supposed to

Unlike fairytales, I can't follow orders from this world

This planet built on billions of mysteries

Transcribed into biblical years

The Man-God, in our book

Couldn't know *this* side of Himself

I had always a theory about the earths beginning

Lectured with Darwin science

Christians attending public schools

That learning against beliefs

Even if the professor was devoted

Classes taught me, division, about ideas

Skin color, political ladders

All needed to know about the secret of life trapped inside this world

I wish I had written an original project

Learning on what could be understood from many *alone* nights

Having spent hour money for my late education

Studying the sound of the AC running

That angry, and love writing on the wall

Those felt-ink pen tags also on the desks, dressers, my elbows had to rest on

I sit back thinking of pin-point thoughts of the ceiling sky

I light a cigarette

Drink just enough

To let loose

Shrink a talk with the minds wall

Lay back on a desk chair

Write about the past

Write and write...

Then after I'm done understanding

I burn down the motel

☐

Desperate times

Stupid clichés

Yet I live by them

Like desperate times

Living for desperate callings

Calling outgoing calls

Desperate for incoming pleasures

I need to get my bottom half wet

Work was overwhelming

My professional colleagues kept me excited

Them smiling, passing them hip hallways

The hospital didn't pay me too much

Because I was in debt for their attention

Fuck it, I went to the Northside of Long Beach

Picked out from a row of dirty mini skirts

Choosing from a line of Z-list actresses

My job had just paid me

I had to rent me a couple of women

Careers

Well, I tried to apply

To be a model

My resume had egotistic standards

Sway, flamboyant, important move references

My pictures showed some chiseled muscles

Goochie, educated trimmed eyebrows

Hickie's not showing, from the night before

The last time I thought I had a job

Was the first time I fell in lust

Just promising myself time

I have the housekeeper

Clean the dust off the floor

Someone cursed this rug

With rock-bottom death-row powder potion

Fiscally irresponsible

Damn

Again, I forgot to pay the bills

Forgot to pay the landlord

Forgot to pay the church

Forgot to pay myself

Forgot that, 'freedom' still charges me

What I won't forget, is my real self

Remembering that beer is my favorite taste

Reminiscing dangerous times interpreted as fun

Rewinding purpose in my brain movie tapes

Rehearsing lines when drinks and drugs chose the words

Revolving around thug normal beings

Relating to dates not important

Damn do I know it

Reminding myself of the debt

I only owe myself

☐

Loyalty

I don't make promises to this world

In this world

Carrying my genetic values

Protecting my everlasting files

Fronting for my favorite vices

Leaving me eventually with no choices

But to die with burden treasures

Gold thoughts need to be gardened

Need to be wanted, harnessed

If I couldn't finish the project

It must stay, where I found it

Behind these treacherous glaring seed brows

Still, I will keep in a vault

Keep those thoughts

Never to be found

The one, finding those

That keep hurting me in the afterlife

Well, you know…

Having me leaving them, written inside,

a Will

☐

Simple trade

My written feelings stacked on a gold bank note

Stashed on top of a fortune

Beneath, became the only trade I could make

Gel maps mysterious to pirates

I bought a notebook

Rough-drafted a document

Printing in word

Nothing different of a treasure map

☐

The way to your heart

Bubble comments spit out chewing gum

She still looks delicious

Ambitious is she

But feels lazy around me

I tell her to focus on the road

But she's still mad at me

Because I didn't buy a rubber

"I couldn't afford it", I tell her

She slaps my face with her bare ass

Thinking to myself

'Yea, that's what I thought'

After parking, to fuck

☐

Chaos

I am brave enough to lose my mind

Because…

This place doesn't make sense

I'm rebellious enough to lift two fingers up

And still, actually care

But still, fuck this place

This place I love to hate

I hate to love

Yes, indeed

But just like farmers

I keep planting my seeds

In this dirty place…

This fucking place

Growing on me

Loving my hatred

That gives me offspring

☐

Long Beach Blvd

Today I took a ride in the rain

L. A., always cloudy

With pollution figures in the sky

It was nice to see clear droplets for a change

The mood in the city was gloomy

But I was feeling happy

Having nature's tears touching my cheeks

The palm trees narrowed down the ocean

As I cruised towards St. Mary's

Reaching the beach

Clear as alkaline water

Went down my throat

But I knew it was toxic

Menthol

Mint cigarettes taste better than gum

Yes

Blowing off cool steam

Is better than caffeine

Let me show you a ghost

After lighting this puff

☐

Thoughts of a Judas goat

Follow *it* like you're a reader

Don't lose track of *it*, like a CD

Listen to *it*, like your favorite playlist

Hold *its* hand, like child pedestrians

Don't lose track

I beg of you

That song you memorized

Becomes the next drug needle

Injected into your soul-stream

Dreaming of many perfect scenarios

Screaming on invisible microphones

On stages, inside your shower

When the music is over

You wake up to rude reality

Expecting the lyrics and melody

To somehow change your weather

For the best

Else you memorize another song anchor

Keeping you replaying the same minutes

Sinking deeper and deeper

Deep underneath pitch black memories

Over and over

Over and over, over and again over

Meanwhile, not knowing the circle of life

Keeps going

Even after the damage is done

Your fault

For scratching the surface too much

Now thin ice

I hope you *see* a way out

Or get stuck, alive

Inside a rabbit hole

Just six feet underground

Just in a choke holding playground

Just in a cycle of tunes

Running out of batteries

Dying before finishing

That best part of the song

That last line

Meant to keep your mind *dreaming*

Dreaming, and sleeping

Sleeping, and repeating

Misery as a meaning

Oh well

Nothing the Judas goat can do

But play the beats to your heart

As you follow the line

Into the butcher's castle

Following the line of other loud dreamers

Don't worry, maybe this time you will wake up

To rich reality

At just the cost of your meat

Better you me than, *it*…

☐

Wait

Floyd Mayweather is the best example of waiting

Just like his belly jabs

Heels up, too quick

Forward with straight right-hands

A hop back

To see you swing silly

A knock-out

If you disrespect him

Pick and choose

His is next movements

Is he

'A fight with Pacquiao is a goldmine,

I think I'll just wait', thought he

And waiting in thinking

He did

50 million back then was too cheap

But after all these years

It was Floyd's time

Taking 100 million, plus interest

On top of that

The world would label it:

'The Fight of The Centry'

☐

Ink

Let me think of something

I can needle to my body

Something extraordinary

Fascinating, like fortune cookies

I just hope I'm not drinking

Deep, on top of my skin

I must tattoo inner ingredients

Some symbol, or writing

Something powerful to cope with the pain

To love the slicing, poking, ink

The meaning must be healthy nutritional

Must represent something original

Must forever bruise a self-inflicted self-description

Must never break the promise of the meaning

So, it must be something

Something I won't forget

Something needed to describe myself

Some hero human being with a non-heart

Something biblical...

How about the initials of my favorite villain

Pontius Pilate

☐

Thoughts of the lamb

Everyone is heading towards the circle

I'm glad it's not a circus

Round and round, my eyes follow

This entertainer contains my amusement

By the end of the show

I will feel bad for the elephant

In the room…

In the other hand, he looks handsome

Especially with that goatee

And that silly white cylinder gentleman hat

With a large star in the middle

Looking more patriotic, than a circus showman

I'm glad I'm not racing towards his pointing fingers

Maybe he'll notice I pay slow attention

Maybe he'll notice I have cheap desires

Maybe he'll take me out

If I remain humble behind the line

What if I cut ahead of the line

Behind, ahead, shouldn't make a difference

Behind my ear I'm whispered, *don't do it*

Well, what does anyone know

He notices me

Notices I don't tip the other servants, looking like rodents

I think he likes me

I can't tell

His tears express sad happy

Or something else

Anyways, I'm next in line

Per hour work

You know details

Maybe don't

Maybe don't care

But the per hour system

Doesn't work

I mean, its mean

Chaining us to economical labor

Stripping off important hours

Firing you on the spot

If your attitude isn't spotless

All from corporate salary decisions

From making honest mistakes

Left to question our life's work

Has it been minimal or grandeur

To the scale of time

Putting more sand work on the right good

Less leverage sand on my left seconds

It's all good

Whether internal verdict in my mind's courtroom

Convicts me or not

I still show up in front of the boss judge

On my last day of work

Whether I quit, or they fire me

I wear a shirt displaying real word objections

"Only God can judge me"

☐

Whitney

My first girlfriend was white

Unlike Houston

She liked me

Even though she stood tall

Hovering five inches over me

"You like me, don't cha?"

She asks me in fifth grade

"Yes, I do", I say shy, facing down the class table

"You know, my best friend likes you", she replies

"Yes, I know, but she's too heavy to push on

the swing set", I blurt out

"You, asshole!"

She looks at her friend across the classroom

Then at me, thinking, 'You know what, I think I might just
like you'

AM line

Simple fact of life

If you don't know something so comforting strange about your eyes

It is this

They are the same size from when born

To the last wrinkles of time

Let's begin a life chapter then

Dot. Dot. Dot.

Comma, comma, comma

Living in this rental corpse the soul is studying subjects

Touching confusing objects

Experiencing curious delirious

The ghost trapped behind the windowsill of our pupils

Is trapped after all

But we choose not to understand

Anyways, mothers breakfast still smells delightful

I cup my chin with my only ten finger sins that know me

Which accepts far too many years

Which has me missing blurry innocent cries

Which has me willing an essay

Which keeps me in life's line

The best is yet to be tasted...

The wait of my eyes was worth it

It is

It must

Because I'm up next

For another expression of coffee

☐

Huddle

Limelight in your eyes isn't familiar

Brother, you better go get another job

Or stick to your expensive writing

I'm serious

I alone can't pay for this rental

This apartment costs a fortress

What happened to you brother

When did you forget the sportsman inside you

Who stole the limelight shining over you

Where did you last feel the excitement

Why did you decide to quit, inches from the goal line

I'm sorry if I hurt your feelings

But excuse me, I am not your momma

Or daddy, who by the way isn't here

What you see around you now

In this moment

Is all you have

So fuckin hell, get back in the game!

And play to win!

Touchdowns came at a risk brother

You know that better than me

You know you were a killer in cleats

You know long ago

You wrote down cheat-sheets

You know right now, you need me

And I do you, so let's put on back your helmet

And get back to work!

Feel sorry for yourself, if you want

But not until we score!

☐

Purple Cush

I can't feel my feet

I'm floating…

Blueberry green is good

But not like purple Cush

It gives you a bed on top of the cloud

With incense of cloudy seaweed

It gives you the time to think, without thinking

It gives off some beautiful aroma out your mouth

It gives you friends

Friends of forever

Repeating quotes like, "I can't wait until tomorrow, but at the same time, I don't want tonight to end."

Anyways, we keep talking too much

I'm dry thirsty

Please pass me the toke

☐

Global warning

My fighting coach doesn't believe in the world fuming

Flames around Quincy could not convince him

Politics had gotten to him

But he was my coach

I listened, agreeing mutually against his mitts

Disregarding my oxygen

My dreams, burning visions

Forgetting about little me

All because coach kept preoccupied with,

Self-researching

Self-reflection

Self-forgetting

Self-obsession

Self-tangled in a worldly web

I was gladiator young to speak

I couldn't tell if he understood my predicament

Or if he was just feeling *self-sorry*

Whatever I learned from him

Whatever my bloody dollars paid for

Reasons for being a madman with a broken nose

Came down through the toughness of his lectures

The lessons taught by my first golden gloves coach

I will never forget about his number one rule

"Fall in love with the pain"

His words aged with respect

Especially now, during rough times

As my world globe eyes

Keeps burning me down

☐

The good die young

I'm a nice guy

Trying to finish first

Cutting in front of the line

Like canine smelling goods

I stay away from innocent addicts

Like me

Finding fresh human produce

In many worldly isles

In good apple eyes, mixed with *us* rotten

Ready for sale

When life police find me

Cuffs tight around my wrists

Admitting white flag murmurs

'Fine, I'll do the time'

'And pay the fine'

'Fine, I won't cut in front again'

'And stay equal like parallel lines'

'Just make sure the stubs

Have my hours amounting correct

And not a penny less'

'Else I'll commit to another crime'

'This time, I'll raise the interest'

'And tax the economy a higher rate'

For telling lies, so beautifully

Showcasing upper and lower cases

Periods, and questions of emotions

Lines stacked on lines

Made in a lab, carefully from my legal life

The vulnerable, and evil side

That part of me I won't remember

So, buy my book or e-book

So, I can continue my criminal school

Get educated, so next time

The police life

Comes for me, to serve me a sentence

I can reply

"I own the judge and the apples

Without me, your worldly isles

Won't sell *rotten* good people"

The *good* stay content

Never *mean* enough

To try and finish first

Fight night

How could I forget fight night...

Two weeks before weigh-in

I was 15 pounds over the weight limit

I needed to make weight, so I decided

Since it was the Golden Gloves

That I would take whatever fat ounce of my skin

To make the right kind of mean self-made muscles

To finally take a fight

It was now or never
Anything to shred off them extra sins
Taking my mind to dehydrated levels...

Never understanding everyday love

Like the *want* of a mother's hug

Like the need of revenge

Like whatever it takes for taking a beating

Like losing myself inside a squared circle

Like it won't matter if I'm being honest

Like dyeing for eating them extra donuts

Like the taste of mountain dew

I was so lonely around my teammates, coaches

Not wanting to show my hungry, vulnerable side

I kept it all inside...

Even during the fight

Not truly expressing myself then

Yet still, I was *Fight of the Night*

Don't believe me

Look up 2018 Tacoma Weekly

Washington State Golden Gloves

☐

Agenda

Specific goals in mind need to be noted

Written and repeated, like a bucket list

Loved and wanted, like a wish list

Invest in this year's planner

Set due dates for your ambitions

Giving your vision a test

When so

A mental mission of war is secretly declared to the Universe

A battle against yourself, to quiz self-limits

Fight, orchestrate

Refine bullet points

Load up in ambitious nutrition

So you can shit all over the enemy

Paper motivation

I wake up every morning

Again, and again

Sometimes hungry

Sometimes hungover

Sometimes angry for considering my alarm clock as my best friend

Sometimes happy I still don't go limp

Sometimes for the fuck of sometimes

Sometimes not sure about anything

Sometimes alone in my thinking

Sometimes forgiving old girlfriends

Sometimes forgetting yesterday

Sometimes obsessed with questions

Sometimes just answering everything else

Too many times I can't even sleep in

Earths young trees must have grown inside a copy machine because...

I remain motivated by piles of papers

By digital ink, noting self-worth

By spring leaving promising green dreams

But emails keep reminding my paper heartbeats of every second

My tombstone will be the receipt

Engraved below my name

Are quotes to the worms

"The earth must continue to charge me

For 'acting' a part in this world"

Am I going to make it?

Probably, probably not

Oh well, fuck it

I'm just going to jump off this cliff

Dive into salty oceans

Take a ride without insurance

Spontaneously define rebellious

Get something expensive

Tip 20 to another life waiter, waiting like me

Expecting that extra change can buy time

Suspecting politeness comes with a price

Exchanging hard earned righteous karma

Accepting that no one really knows

Why the gamble clock is broken

Still, I put my pocket change on me

Like I do, with others waiting in lottery lines

This time, though...

Whether the drinks, or my generosity

I tip another 20

Not sure why

I don't want to remember

Probably it must be done

Just to feel important

Alien heritage

Growing up, my folks were called illegal aliens

Because they were in the States illegally

Living honestly

Giving life to four legal babies

My sibling and I didn't understand the system

At the time

We thought it was weird to know two languages

Unlike the whites

Though most times confusing when trying to understand each other

Trying to explain the teachers and others

Vacations during summertime wasn't real

Out of school meant a few months of working in the fields

With fake documents, papers, security numbers

To let our tiny innocent hands claim older than eighteen for a check

Working alongside many adult aliens

By the end of the week

We were happy to keep ten dollars

Having no idea about the meaning of money

Having no idea about back then, modern day slavery

Clocking in and out

For many years

Now...

School, work, college, then work again

Sure, I'm happy for these moments

Most times

But I sure would like to understand more about the choices chosen for me

Back then, when vacation wasn't too fun

Then maybe I could know more about myself

And my alien heritage

☐

Quotes

"Everything happens for a reason"

Is the worst fuckin quote

Along with its cousin

"There is no such thing as coincidence"

Like why the fuck say these things

I'll tell you why

It is because of people like you

Those couple quotes manage to combine

The maximum lie of arrogance

Just isolate yourself with another quote

"It's all part of the 'great' plan"

How about, let's find out

If those beliefs form content situations

Or if they betray

My original saying, quoted by me

"*Love,* is a willful willing negligence, isn't it? Some *truths,* are just meant to be questions."

Mother earth

Every day we hear complaints from CNN and Fox

Reading prompts of national chaos

Politics and immigrants

Being their main event arguments

So, propaganda from the real controllers of the world

Continue to fulfill a prophecy only they can know

Ear anchors talking about war superstitions

Whose right or wrong on the ballot

Who to vote via survey polls

Idiots, all idiots

Father-time idiots

We ignore her pain

Her suffering

Our species of free-minded souls

Also ignore that her belly core

Will explode sooner than we think

Think about it

We have taken, and keep taking the oil beneath ground

Beneath the oceans

Sucking up the gelatin joints of her structure

Fuck

We are fucked

For not filling in the holes

Those questions are left for the next generation

I swear

It will still haunt us

Because father-time will still call us idiots

Meanwhile, mother nature does her best

Giving us shade, under her tree caress

Serious

I keep thinking about something curious

Like something I'm missing

Like diving deep high feelings

Like forgetting I'm nothing

Like, unlike many people I like

Like the media making me jealous

Like your life, making me envious

Like, I can't like you

If you're taking me *serious*

☐

Safe suicide

A way out is easy

Like a shot

To forget about existing

Like a shot

Quick smooth drinking

Like a shot

Slow thinking memoirs

Like a shot

Shutting the lights out

Powder in the bullet is the same as dirt dust

To take my bones back home

To Gods landfill

Misery has become my fortress

Mysteries of feelings locked in some castle

My queen is a fairytale

My princess is nonsense

My prince is some pen

My loyalty scripts soldier ink-men

Rewriting wills, again and again

Until *love* inheritance, has me executed

☐

Baby Boy
Ralph, the man, the dad, the example

I met Mr. Ralph in my early 20's

Working for an assisted living facility

He was a tough, grumpy, rocky, happy, sour man

Mornings weren't his greatest during breakfast

Of course, because his age rounded close to 100

But his soul, celebrated 21st birthdays

Maybe as his caregiver, he told me confidentially

About the roots of his life

A social investigator, after surviving war times

I wasn't aware of the beacon heart in front of me

How could I, his light years later made my writing possible

Back then, I listened but still sorting out my feelings

Young and wrong

In my choices, because I chose to judge no one

Like now, but this is what I felt from Mr. Boyd

Ralph, thank you for the opportunity

May I speak your mind:

Maybe mother had her excuses, who knows

Success, failure, death, I can't help but to just miss her

A long rope of questions, was detached from my umbilical cord

Only time will answer my investigations

Trying to understand the truth about himself:

Maybe dad carried a burden he couldn't share with himself

Perhaps mother was too young to love

Investigating these self hollows is keeping me tired

Closing the Heavens Gate answers

These decades of sub-thoughts searching

Have put me in a bottom lost floor

I need to float back up

Be an example

My daughter, granddaughters, need me

Mom, dad

I hope to see you soon

For now, I will be Ralph Boyd

A forgiving choice, I'm choosing to be...

And he did just that

Legally knowing himself as Ralph

A tough militant

Sharp, smart, intriguing individual

He may, or may have not figured out life's answers

But as far as his love knew

Through his sweetheart wife and roots

He is the one and only

Original

Baby Boy, as written on his birth certificate

Blogging drunk
Did I blog this?

Fuck, I must had been drunk

Actually, I usually was

When I opened the app

To pour on baby ink tears into a worldwide canvas

In the moment it all screams *badass*

Then the next day when my left hemisphere brain part

Decides to spellcheck for me

It ends up doing overtime

Re-typing glob words

Fitting them correctly for the unseen internet world of writers

Both spheres of my world don't often agree on the paper-lined platform

Transcribing the right combination emotions

Locked-linked inside my pains

Those pains are easy to exploit when drunk

Those suspense moments are easy to publish

Those silent questions are easy to yell

Those old scar wounds are easy to open

Those explicit ink tears made of my years

Is meant to stay sane to myself

I guess I've become a drunkard blogger to be honest because

My left-hand side can't write for shit

☐

Nothing gold can glow

Reservations, combinations, secret passwords

Are all stored, in the 'federal reserve'

This nation needs to make sure we keep climbing up status

A social exchange

An economy life preference

Europeans struck the idea first

Revolutions, killing civil compass cities

Promising to be the police of this planet

Even after back-to-back World War Wins by the *U. S.*

The next showdown

Will be the greatest

Enemies wanting our blood

Wanting our rights

Wanting our freedom

Wanting our gold

I keep, and keep investing

Our forefathers took too many bloody coins

Religious rebellions

With faith of fireworks

Saluting a theme song

Strong enough

To keep Christian hearts

Beating, and eliminating the weak

Protecting our nations forefather's soul

Our, Federal Reserve

The fight in her heart

She was sick that morning

And all week

Leading up to a Holy day that weekend

A fever, cough, delusions

All transpired to what I needed to bear witness

Too that, Holy night

Maybe others saw it

Maybe no one caught it

Maybe everyone was lost in robe literature

While I was creating innocent memories

For a 'maybe'

Because what I saw as child, in her

Was the devil laughing inside the Temple

Those eyes twisted right towards me

I couldn't believe that crooked smirk

Crossed across my *dear* one

I became scared of such meaning

That I needed to look away

Next thing that happens, she feints

Her husband and family pick her up

She's tired, too tired, so tired, angry tired

God, and the devil must continue to wrestle

For her spirit

Her wounded soul

All the while

She must wait

For that one question

That one answer

Reserved, to set her free

Time will tell...

Looking up with eyes of help

Lips of trespass

She asks

"If I have learned to forgive, how come I still don't know *love* yet?"

☐

The end

After reading and listening to me

What do you think?

Hopefully nothing

Because, "hope", I left for you to be free

In your thoughts of pictures and symbols

Don't forget you felt a certain pillar with me

But think out loud to me

Did your eyes and mouth full of letters

See beauty or royalty?

Don't waste my time answering

Every single human body is a walking, talking curse

But I've learned to love them

The world in my mind is like professor X

Engage in my words to control it

The letters to re-form, re-program, re-write

Or delete it

Could your writing on a blank page

Be the key to let go

That gripping squeeze

That freeze, that stone-cold

Soap opera that's part in your soul

Who knows

But when do you want to know?

Imagine your own life show

Then you get bored

Complain when the audience walks out the theater

Because your acting became ridiculous

Too much obsession in questions

Too much regretting 'staying'

Too much truth in your lies

Too much of too much of never enough

Typing and writing
Your eyes made of experience is ink made of gold
Bubble words of your thinking, and doing defines
The role of your footprints
By the end of your sentence
I hope you rehearse, and rehearse

Tell me your favorite last words
Before the warden of the world
Symbols your end.

Made in the USA
Las Vegas, NV
24 March 2024

87707414R00095